BESIDE THE
HEMLOCK GARDEN

ON LIVES AND RIGHTS

The moonlit water
An idle reflection
Are we dead already?
We've yet to be alive

BESIDE THE
HEMLOCK GARDEN

—— ON LIVES AND RIGHTS ——

JAMES STRECKER

mosaic press

National Library of Canada Cataloguing in Publication Data

Strecker, James - 1943
        Beside the hemlock garden / James Strecker.

Poems.
ISBN 0-88962-793-2

        I. Title.

PS8587.T72335B4 2002   C811'.54   C2002-903523-6
PR9199.3.S8355B4 2002

Published by Mosaic Press, offices and warehouse at 1252 Speers Road, Units 1 and 2, Oakville, Ontario, L6L 5N9, Canada and Mosaic Press, PMB 145, 4500 Witmer Industrial Estates, Niagara Falls, NY, 14305-1386, U.S.A.

Mosaic Press acknowledges the assistance of the Canada Council and the Department of Canadian Heritage, Government of Canada for their support of our publishing programme.

Mosaic Press in Canada:
1252 Speers Road, Units 1 & 2,
Oakville, Ontario
L6L 5N9
Phone/Fax: 905-825-2130
mosaicpress@on.aibn.com

Mosaic Press in U.S.A.:
4500 Witmer Industrial Estates
PMB 145, Niagara Falls, NY
14305-1386
Phone/Fax: 1-800-387-8992
mosaicpress@on.aibn.com

Le Conseil des Arts   The Canada Council
du Canada   for the Arts

www.mosaic-press.com

DEDICATION

In a significant way, encounters with each of the following inspired or encouraged this book to come into existence:

In Canada: *Margaret Strecker, Ann Tantala, Gérard Dion, Sharon FitzSimon, Victoria Mihalyi, Max Miller, Regan Russell, Anne Doncaster, Michael Schwab, Joanne Schwab, Joanna Chapman, Jean Rumney, Marie-Lynn Hammond, Diane McCarthy, Cassandra Prince, Diane Esther, Karin England, Liz White, Ainslie Willock, Harold Town, Kathie Hunter, Michael Horwood, Wolfgang Bottenberg, Farley Mowat, Michael FitzSimon, Kevin McEvenue, Anton Kuerti.*
In the United States: *Polly Strand, Alka Chandna, Ira Progoff, Bina Robinson, Isaac Bashevis Singer, Valerie Harms, Ingrid Newkirk, Dan Matthews, Philip Glass, Gretchen Wyler, Loretta Swit, Jello Biafra, Cleveland Amory, Mark Braunstein, Beth Nielsen Chapman.*
In Europe: *Jon Wynne-Tyson, Jan Creamer, Hans Ruesch, Chrissie Hynde, Chris Murphy, Jeremy Brett, Martin Carthy, Hayley Mills, Barend Schipper.*

To them, or to their memory, this book is gratefully dedicated

A C K N O W L E D G E M E N T S :

Some of the poems in this present collection appeared
most recently in the books *Bones to Bury* (1984), *Cork-
screw* (1986), *Recipes for Flesh* (1989), *Echosystem* (1993),
Animal Matters (1996), *Foundations of English* (2001) *and
Golden Horseshoes* (2002); in *The Hamilton Spectator*
(1997); on the CD-ROMs *Literature: A Practical Approach*
(1997) and *Walking Alone* (1999); in *Michael Horwood's
Symphony #2: Visions of a Wounded Earth* (1995); in
Wolfgang Bottenberg's composition Recipes for Animals(nd);
on *Barend Schipper's CD Three Classical Savages on Music*
(1998); in the *program of the Ark Trust's Genesis Awards*
(1994); in the *Margie Gillis souvenir program*(1995); and
at the *Fashion Shares* evening of the *Hamilton Aids Net-
work* (1994).

Partial funding for this book was generously provided by
Polly Strand.

Special thanks to the courageous and always inspiring
Sue Coe for her painting for the cover.

C ONTEN T S

Photo by Dave Sage

P REFAC E

Albert Camus, in *The Rebel*, challenges his reader with this blunt assertion: "He who despairs over an event is a coward, but he who holds hopes for the human condition is a fool."

With this observation of Camus in mind , it indeed seems both cowardly and foolish to publish a book of poetry imbued with despair and an occasional, albeit fragmentary, optimism. Indeed, a book, after all, is only a book and the world goes on with its madness.

Nonetheless, there is purpose in the following pages of poems, taken from my seven previous collections, poems about animal abuse, human brutality, hard-earned brief happiness, and lives without any rights. The poems were written to foster awareness first in the author and then, of course, the reader. What this book describes must be known since denial of what goes on in the world every day can be a greater curse than despair. When we choose to be unaware, others suffer and we, despairing or not, are less for it.

And hope? Because a naïve hope, by its very nature, certainly denies, we must welcome awareness of our place in the world. We must give hope a substance that first acknowledges our nature and our deeds before we dream of a nobler species in ourselves. We must earn our hope.

A few years ago I mentioned to Philip Glass, the composer, how hard it was sometimes to find shoes not made of leather. He responded, "It's harder for the animals if we don't." And so be it with the poems that follow. One finds little respite here, but, in the end, the reader's escape is not the issue, since so many who suffer elsewhere have no hope of escape. In the end, one can despair or take hope but, at the peril of one's humanity, it is not an option to be a complacent or a stupid witness to a world one might try to change.

James Strecker, September 2002

Of Course, I Heard Voices

Of course, I heard voices,
lamentable voices too frenzied in their
bleeding for my complacent wisdom.

It's the healer who is healed, they said,
the lover who is blessed in honest love.

But they spoke verbatim to silence when
I asked for more than an answer of them.
Shall the killer be killed?
But, by then, it was only my voice.

Of course, I heard voices, the moan
of cattle broken twisted at the knee
and, skin on stone, dragged by chains,

or the squealing pig skinned in motion
like an evil ballet, or the chicken blithering
confusion until hand-broken at the neck,

or you, of unspoken voice, who knew this
wilful cruelty and made no sound. Of
course, I heard voices; there were many
loud, unbearable voices to hear.

A Trapper's True Story

I once was a trapper
and where I made footsteps
I echoed a shadow of blood.

I gripped every season with
my bare hands and did what I
had to do, sometimes more,

though I knew I would die
and lie naked underground,
my skin like every winter's ice.

One day, as I checked my
lines, I walked into a clearing
where morning unveiled amazing
pure light. I knew myself more

than alive and, that very instant,
I saw the mother fox in my trap.

She'd been nursing her kits, four
of them, while my jagged vice
cut into her flesh to the bone;

she'd been crazy with fear and pain,
I could tell, for there was much
blood spattered all around.

And as I walked toward the vixen,
she raised her head to watch me
come through the clearing. And she

gently picked up each of her
young by the neck, one at a time,
and lay her child close to her breath
and licked her milk from its face,

and snapped its neck. She did that
to all four before I could reach her.

And as she watched me over her
newly born, over her dead she had
saved from my hands, I knew
I would never trap again. And I

never have, though I killed her
with one bullet as she lay back
waiting to die. I buried the mother

and her fur, and tonight, in the
warming nighttime of spring, I wonder
if ever I'll sleep until morning again.

THE AUTUMN OF KNOWLEDGE

You are the autumn of knowledge.
The earth omens everlasting dark winter.
You must gather your bloodlines of reason,
and be silent what logic would pray.

You must drag your parched and eloquent
tongue upon dead waters, and know your
heart a demon of your very own making.

It is spoken among the crevices, where
you presume shelter, that your bondage is all
places. Your grave protests in heartbeat,
your heartbeat, but only an arid

reflection, scented with darkness, speaks
to condemn no greener place for you to die.
You have known the earth holy, but killed

her new-born grasses, as if you knew
comfort in the ruin you made, and
ravaged a purpose made of no beginning,
a purpose you could not see.

But I do not bring you here to prove you
evil or mad, for you are witness to another
truth never born of your deeds. You are
diseased and nothing you shall ever understand.

Yet beware this solitary branch seducing you
still. It will lure you to the edge of the sky and
there you shall babble, grateful and unafraid.

There, your time shall be dust, like the earthly
dust you betrayed, until the coldest infinity hears
silence where your dangling footsteps shiver.

MASAI MARA

The wildebeest flow
to Masai Mara,
burst from Serengeti.
A lion, still as vapour
in the grasses,
watches over
the gnu's hungry surge
for another place.
He waits
with absolute balance,
a planet
in outer night. Death
and twilight
wait their turn
beside the feline
predator.

A rancid sky
when someone dies,
milked of dignity.
Perhaps you understand
though what we know
is not the same. I
eat no meat,
kill in not killing.
And powerless to heal,
ten dreadful steps
from a lion
whose paw
might crush my throat,
I give the lion leeway,
not man.

Kenya, 1980

THE DANCER
for Kimberly Glasco

The truth night speaks upon her flesh
denies her mystery. Yet a dream unfolds
the dancer's heart once more, like a star,
of no confusion, that knows she must be.

She is elegance made of certainty, born
as she dances, and nothing born of time;
when the moon lays fingers on her dance,
she is made of her beginning.

Like a vein of unknown dimension,
she dances a sorrow made of ecstasy,
a balance of will and the moonless sky,
and her grace bows seamless like the wind.

For a moment, some burning ache of light
burns steady and gentle through her,
perhaps the source of all fire in her fusion
of whispering wounds and summer air.

Yet each summer of the earth blooms most
alive in snow, although we know the seasons
because we give them names. So her beauty too
is yes and no; she will disappear, if we look away.

Our secret wilderness makes us what we are,
but if we are amazed, we've become amazing too.
I know her without knowledge, for she has never
been; and yet this sadness too shall dance again.

A Doctor Describes His Work

I tarred some of the dogs
and set fire to them. I
disembowelled others and

poured boiling water into
the cavity. I held their
paws over a blowtorch.

I crushed the testicles of
some male dogs. I broke all
the bones of their limbs.

I gouged out the eyes of
some dogs and scraped the
orbits. In others, I

manipulated the intestines.
I poured ether into the
windpipe. I shot one with

a .38 pistol, another with
a .32 pistol. I manipulated
the kidneys of one dog, then

its liver, then I inflicted
a serious injury to one of
its kidneys, then I shot

it with a .32 pistol. I
used 148 dogs to study
surgical shock. I used

incomplete anaesthesia.
In this year of 1899,
George W. Crile, physician.

WORLD DAY FOR LABORATORY ANIMALS
for Jan Creamer

If the vivisection lab were made
of glass, a crowd as large as humanity
would witness, eager, uneasy, and curious
outside. Some would call the deed
torture, vindictive, not science, and
some would call the deed thinking
without a soul. And some would name
death their one desire, for this world
of perfect knowledge is truly hell.

Yet as each season dies into the birth
of another, and we of false serenity still
burn our hands to clutch the sun, our
mercies endure, though we are passion
and dust. For without compassion, we
are nothing, only mortal. With mercy,
we are more than alive: we are footsteps,
we are sound, and we seek not science
but greater knowing. And thus we know

that every god dwells divine within the
living flesh of rats and mice, of rabbits,
cats and dogs, and within every he and
she alive. This is not news, this is
common knowledge, even among the
dead, the tortured and the dead we mourn
here today. If we speak no language to
describe the precise and gutless cruelty
intended by women and men, we can

never be still, for, in our multitude
purpose, even one life may be spared: in
this brief mercy, only mercy is true.

London, April 25, 1992

JAMES STRECKER

In The Waiting Room

I would have you stand
on some green elevation
where sun-clouds might shatter
the wounds that made you wounded.
But you are dying and I flee into silence
from your help me, help me eyes,
you whose sperm poured blood into mine
until I learned of your callused radiance
as we also wounded each other.

Perhaps I shall bend with wisdom
over your body and ache my untried silence
that knows no regard for time, whimper
perhaps turned away from your stone-quiet,
untormented peace because you once
taught me, "Don't tell them you saw me
cry." I shall beat my thinking with anger
and fist, and count the ways we ran from
each other and pulled, with angry love,
the chains of flesh that kept us bound. And I too
shall die in time with no more fire, no remedy.

Beside you I have walked into music
and come out a changed man, walked among
trees and heard the things of this world tell
me what they are. Like you, I have run
from my loneliness and, in running, found
myself more lonely. Still, you loved your
family and gave what you had: love made
of scars and innocence, love made of sunlight
and fields of wheat, love scented with brandy
that beat us into confusion, and always a
desperate love when this world of butchers
dismembered your heart from your dreams.

WORDS FOR A FRIEND
In memory of Harold Town

On a sun-singing spring afternoon,
a day scented with gutsy colours
you've painted four decades or more,
a spring day, yes, but cold,
cold and mean enough for sidewalk ice,

the damp wind elbows through
your bushes outside
and I see you and hear you
panic in glances and words,
panic the way the newly helpless do:
you know you'll be dead
before you are well again.

Still, we talk of painting, poems,
women, music, the farm,
and, as usual, everything else,
then we verbally piss on a critic or two,
and as I leave,
and before you close the door,
you say, "I love you, buddy,"
and your artist hands are ruined
from chemotherapy.

Now another day,
I bring you my poem
written for your birthday
and we sit to watch the trees
you planted greening,
greening into summer as you die.
And you say, "I wouldn't
have worried as much,"
and we conclude together
that animals have souls
while some men don't. But you are dead

and my heart speaks to your ashes,
scattered where we, grown kids,
rode your fire engine together,
scattered smaller than dust.
The sky today seems clouded with the sun
and part of me is dust with you
and part of me is born in my grief,
but the wound of your dying
hurts still too much
because time takes time.

Harold, you are dead but three weeks:
would you believe that men
have become even more lunatic?
All we love is in danger forever
and maybe what we need to save us
won't show. Yet in spite of this world,
because of it, you painted what few,
save you, could imagine. I loved
your art and came to love you,
my friend, its maker.

Harold, on Bloor Street yesterday
I watched a young woman,
the kind we used to notice.
There was something unreachably crazy
in her waiting to happen
and her skin whispered flesh
like the lines you drew.
Then I watched your thousand toy horses
take over city hall at last
and I wished like hell I could phone you
and tell you all about it.

ANIMALS

Sunset belongs to animals.
They know each darkness;
they weave the language of shadows.
Their footsteps echo sun in the moon,
like response to an echo responding.

At sunset, I pay heed to my wife.
She lies in her darkness bedded
with cats; she touches her cats
and lays hands on everything I know.
And cats sleep in shelter

through her dream and my own,
our dream that never dares to sleep,
while colour goes blind in the sun's
impeccable hue and all is gift
in this naked haven of the night.

PORPHYRY
for Jon Wynne-Tyson

As Porphyry advised
Firmus, his friend,
to abstain again
from meat's hypnotic
spell, so I advise you

too: consume a gentler
diet and re-ascend the
"realm of the Real"

and purify, approaching
gods, your soul of
foreign nature. Remember
the time when sacrifice
was bloodless offering
of apple and wheat, and

gods desired thus of
man "pure intellect and
impassive soul." I repeat
that man, become more

humane, verges on the
divine, that animals reason
too, though unheard by man,
and urge you to heed
what Pythagoras described:

Bassarians who slaughter
bulls and consume, in
turn, the putrid flesh
of fallen enemies.

IN THE COTSWOLDS

The morning describes
a meadow of stars, stars
brought home to rest in graces
of dew. The sheep seem riveted
to earth, grazing in the fields
overlapping from town to town.
It is beautiful, and then too beautiful,

for the traveller passing by. He
pauses, enchanted, in a music
composed of mounting celestial
light, a radiant light that watches
over sheep sparse as moons. He
feels his heart upside down among
the clouds; he feels the meter of rain.

But his life, by afternoon, is more
a butcher's making. The gentle soul
drives home to eat the lamb he hasn't
killed and, in his untroubled sleep,
remembers the sheep he left in pasture
behind, their blood in his blood,
their slaughter akin to his music.

A Wound

I peeled away my brittle skin; the scab
lay naked, dead. It conjured, for some reason,
a swine with eyes dumbstruck and open wide,
no legs to flee, nor heart to beat existence. I
rubbed it gently, once or twice, to endure the
lingering pleasure of pain, and remembered
how the wounded deal their cards this way:
they harvest their meaning in misery. I

envisioned the swine, naked of skin and not
quite dead, the swine demanding an answer:
Are we worthy of life to love and think we
also have blessing to kill, kill until the world
bleeds no more like a soul that cannot be?

It is no quirk of wisdom that one gentle
hand deceives a beloved flesh, that a brain's
imbecility guides the other hand to destroy.
The spirit that sees a victim meaningless has
already died itself, unholy here and forever. But
who can reason with the dead? Only the dead.

Even so, let me address you as an alien
queen of the mountains, regal and lassie on
your naked toes, the succulent peat soil
between them all. And tell me your passion,
not your modesty, in a singing voice that
knows to bleed. And sing aloud an honest
voice, hopeless on the highest mountain cliff,
a voice that confesses the ways you kill, a
voice of fangs like vibrations of your heart.

GOULD PLAYS BYRD'S
FIRST PAVANE AND GALLIARD

If darkness be light indivisible,
or want of light that conspires
greater darkness, each notion
of art knows no love's fibre.
The moon's dark quarter becomes
another moon, and silences dream

one another among the living, among
the unreachable dead. Even the sentient
stars cannot heal this wound in the
universe; and even those who aspire
with love shall be neither water nor
sky, but silence, veined of silence,
and perfect only because they die.
But in darkness every sound is
true, and imagination, willed or
made of will, flows like cosmic blood
where light is spent. Souls, whatever
they are, overlap on spirit, on the
criss-cross dance of nothing and idea.
We are naked of purpose here, we
carve our meaning in sound, though
music makes no shadow, even in pure
light. Each sound dies superfluous to
silence, dies nothing before our brief
wisdom dies, perfectly this and
imperfectly that, perhaps eternal.

DOCTOR TALK

The intern
describing a nurse
from Jamaica
is overheard: "Once

you've had black meat,
you'll never want
white meat again."

And the woman hearing this
becomes meat,

with meat, maybe cancer,
growing inside her belly.
She listens to the
specialist: "We remove

the baby carriage
but you still keep the playpen.
It takes six months to heal.

She listens to learn
that her body is her life,
listens forever alone,
while fear and reassurance

numb the air,
and the nothing to him
speaks to nothing in her.

A HISTORIAN CONSIDERS HIS LUNCH

On the way to Auschwitz
the train stopped at
a Kentucky Fried Chicken stand.
Four thousand orders were
taken; the short order cook
bitched about the lousy pay.

The train resumed its run
past Polish farmers
harvesting in the field. The
Jews and Gypsies in livestock cars
waved their pieces of chicken
wing and sipped on icy cola
from wax-coated cups,

many had asked for two straws.

Word has it
the cleanup crew who swept
the debris all that night
had a hell of a time. The

floors were a mess: napkins,
withering coleslaw,
and piles of sticky bone
smelling of meat.

LE PONT DES ARTS

From the Pont des Arts,
the Seine flows sovereign to thinking,
forked until married once more
past the Ile St. Louis. It's a river
divided like the human heart's fibre
that opens to embrace a solitary wound,
until, surprised at mercy, it toys
with every cruelty, home-safe again.

On the Pont des Arts, I stand miming
an innocent fool, rain-soaked in ideals
though cold to the skin and despising
humankind. But, mouth agape, taken
by lightning that shapes a celestial
dining fork into Belleville and the Marais,
I find it very hard to describe what
is actually happening, to describe

and not only describe but half a truth.
I remember the Rembrandt painting
of this afternoon, The Flayed Ox: a headless
carcass, stubs for limbs, oils thick as
bloody flesh rendered into masterpiece.
It is a jewel of artifice, but we know
the guts have fallen elsewhere. We ask
what is true, the painting or the animal.

In Rue St. Denis, the herds of men stare
endlessly at doorway whores and sneer
to avenge their need of women. They hate
women, even the blonde, rendered neon
and rouge, who steals my breathing from
her doorway gilded with piss. Are we
human in this? Women despised and sold
near butcher shops where liver and thigh

and tongue decay together. Flesh devours
flesh, consumes it impassive and glad:
no philosophy here, even in Paris where
Descartes took dogs for unfeeling machines.
Tonight, the worms chew Descartes' reason
from his bones and belch up a conclusion
no man can endure, until the worms, like
intellect, are merely a compost for time.

In the Quartier Latin, a restaurant window
displays an altar of death, each part
of anatomy allotted a price: the pig's head
stares stupidly into hungry eyes, while,
slice by slice, her thigh is consumed, cognac
to follow. Who will bind all these pieces
of flesh together again to make one life?
Who will shape these organs and muscles

into one jigsaw puzzle that breathes?
On the Pont des Arts, I hear wine and its
laughter, each man a cup of mortality
that shall empty for all time, a putrid
nothing to no one and forever. And yet
a man loves his cats and dogs, and,
drunk in the groin, he loves his women
too, loves his art to fertilise ennui.

But my thinking tonight is meat,
and man, like every manifestation of
his god, is meat as well. He is butchered
with each day, his blood dried to powder,
his killer killed in turn because he stood
still. And yet it remains very hard
to describe what is actually happening:
the rain clouds flow out of reason

down a heavenly river and the sky
overhead, a luminous mockery of night,
is full of gracious possibility, river-reflected
and reflected in the heart. Then I kill
and you kill and the rain is truly acid
falling down, until one of us kills
and all of us die for it. But enough: the sun
has reappeared if only to set and the city

is what we are: a ruthless, grimy elegance
too merciless for love. In medieval
alleyways, freckled with canine turds
and reeking of urine under three-star
cuisine, the whores' foreplay glances
belittle the hunger in men. Then passion
makes an ass of us, before it truly dies,
over semen, blood, and poems in a sewer.

Hôtel du Vieux Paris, 1987

Epiphany

On a bird-watching
tour to Point Pelee,
a complimentary lunch:

chicken sandwiches

TWO PHOTOGRAPHS

One is a cat, numb in restraint,
and in pain without hope

only science can excuse,
belly up, legs spread

out to each corner,
belly up and ready

for incision to her
nerves: may you

always remember how
her eyes are pleading

to die. The other is
a woman, gagged into

silence, elbows tied
behind her and she is

armless, naked from
her pleading eyes to

ankles clamped down
with bolts, and her

legs spread open at
centre page to show

pussy that someone else,
perhaps a neighbour

next door, also studies
with a dagger.

SUNDAY IN DACHAU

There are photographs
in Dachau: discarded
bodies, hollow stares
of fish on a plate,
lampshades tattooed.

Beyond mute foundations
where barracks stood,
a restaurant cook
renames anonymous flesh,
a tasty, if greasy,
cuisine. Yet patrons

drink blood and know
they're drinking blood.
Over cabbage and wurst
they offer reverent thanks,
a prayer that smells,
it smells of Sunday school.

Dachau, 1969

HE WAS WOUNDS

He was wounds waiting for a knife. No
fiend ran a dagger across his tongue
to make a speechless fool of him; he
stuttered and mumbled quite on his own
and learned to undo his fly. At dusk when
sunset crawled over the waves to welcome
his aching feet, he pissed a rushing golden
arch and marvelled at the rainbow. At
dawn he drank the water. He

was wounds, wounded in slavery.
But no blood dripped from his servile
arm. He cut through his skin every day
and with the advent of night walked
through the hazy scent of pine, pilgrim
to the labourers' camp. No one could
find his blood. The men all took swings
with their axes too and found their blades
as dry as his wounds. He

was wounds awaiting the turbulent
herd, hooves to trample his head
near the barn. Only a workhorse appeared,
a tired mare, weary without any wounds.
The animal would not move. He walked
to the house, picked up his hammer,
and ran to the yard. He beat at her ribs
till she bled with a crack. The wounded
was looking for wounds.

DESIRE

The fur you drape on your shoulder
has no feet. The fox, in a trap,
chewed her foot to the bone, then

died pouring blood through her veins
like an open faucet on snow. The shoes you
dangle on your genteel toes are the skin

of a calf who lived a conveyor belt life.
Without mother or touch of any kind,
she reached for a nipple and was fed a

chemical gruel. Your lipstick was
force-fed down the gullets of mice and
rats until their stomachs distended

in pangs of misery. Your delicate
powder inflated beagle stomachs until
they burst. Even the shampoo that

renders your hair into strands of gold
was dripped into rabbits' eyes until they
went blind and wretched in a bolted vice.

Now as you undress, I desire you.
For a moment, I go crazy in your smell
and follow each strand of hair, on your

shoulder, to a moon beyond the moon. But then
I vomit on your perfumed skin because you
are dead, like all who died for your beauty.

FROM INSIDE THE ZOO CAGE
for Cassandra Prince

Your eyes are born of an evil contemplation. In
your culture of toys, you demean all you see and
claim my existence like a relic in a museum,
curse me to amuse and never defy. I am a prisoner
of war, the war against all life that sired you, and
your children are devils in the making. They too
would break my will and watch to kill me slowly.

When the trees were woman, you cut them down.
You slaughter the Indians still in everything you do
and leave the earth, like miles of buffalo carcass,
to rot and smell. Your own human debris, a
wasteland of rotted ideas, reveals no ghost
behind, nothing remembered, nothing to eat and
chew. But I am no dead artifact; in fact, I breathe
like you. I also despair to walk, endless, back and
forth. But my prison is my salvation, you say.

I dwell within your curiosity, I am a zoo of one.
My life is putrid water, the sun and the cold I
cannot flee, the meager food that tastes of starvation,
and always your eyes, your insane need of needing.
You are miserly with mercy, even with the air you

breathe. Elsewhere, though never again elsewhere,
I might chew off the fingers you point at me, suck
hollow your Big Mac eyes, and feed your precocious
certitude to my young. Elsewhere you might run, if I
were uncaged, where the Kenyan grasses and sky
roll on forever until I hunted you down. In you,
I would kill, for food, the disease that makes you
look on impassive, that makes me nothing. I would
eat to vomit every human so diseased and ponder
how you are strange, too strange for even a zoo.

MILKSHAKE AND OMELETTE

Because the cow's a machine, to suckle
man, not her own, the calf, her child
newly born, is taken away. The female

calf becomes another machine; the male
calf, anaemic veal. Because the mother
gives milk for only ten months,
re-breeding takes place maybe fifty days
after the calf is born. The machine is

greased and oiled, you might say.
The human hand never dirties this
efficient procedure: rubber cups, plastic

tubes, and vacuum pumps extract the
cow's milk. Milk, warm and fresh, then
flows directly to refrigerated tanks
twice a day. The operator needs only to
disinfect the udder, apply suction cups

to the teats, and attend the machinery,
living or stainless steel. Feeding and
water appear automatically, manure is

removed with ease, without offending
stench. Gates open and close by
technological magic. When production
wanes, the cow is sent to a slaughterhouse.
She's a machine, however, and not

graded high enough for steak or filet, but
ground into hamburger for fast-food
chains. The breeding machines who
remain are chained by the neck, on

concrete floors, for many paralysing
months on end.   The hen is also a machine,
beaks and toes clipped away because even
hens will kill their own when locked in

cages piled too efficiently high. Male
chicks don't lay eggs, so the bottom line
decrees they be suffocated in heavy-duty

plastic bags. The hens are confined to
automation when mature. Two conveyor
belts bring feed and collect the eggs, an
easy task because the eggs roll away from
the hens down slanted floors. They are

washed and graded, packed and stored, and
even the chicken droppings are scraped
away by automatic will, untouched by hen

or man. After eighteen months, the profits
each hen produces begin to dwindle. Each
hen, like two hundred and fifty million other
gears in the system, have ground, like
useless rust, to a halt. They are all made

into soup and other processed food.   There
are no psychiatrists employed at a factory
farm, though cows and hens and men

who keep their systems working are
visibly mad or going efficiently crazy. But
the living spare parts remain in endless
supply, to replace the wheels that have
broken down, because these cogs, both flesh
and steel, are nothing but replaceable.

MEN ARE LIKE PIGS

inside a costume rental store
you receive the costume of a pig;
it is loose around the waist

waiting at the slaughterhouse,
you are waiting in line.
no one has been here before

you are killed and dismembered.

the butcher has a sale today.
he is selling your ribs to Eve.
she is driving home with a bag

Eve is making you a stew.
she is cooking dinner in the nude.
she is wearing a costume

THE REWARD FOR NOT EATING MEAT

I admire the way
Miss Laura Antonelli

pays a bimonthly visit
to Toronto

in the nude. Whenever
she's in town

I take off my clothes
and grab a cab

to the Bloor Cinema
for a box of popcorn

and soda with ice. One
day, I prophesy, she'll

descend from the screen,
and rest her ten foot

Technicolor bum
on my lap. Then she'll

whisper, soft as feathers,
in my ear:

"You smella so nice,
you sexy vegetarian!"

A One Room Shack

a one room shack (
they do exist
) in 1946

my mother awoke
to see her gentle hand
become arthritic claw

she yielded the farm
and bore the curse
of barely making

a living. in Washington
she posed her sons
beside the Capitol

preserved their faces
like strawberry jam.
then Hamilton,

choking industrial
fumes, though I try
to believe she simply

inhaled, let the smoke
pass through her
bones without

coagulating. in truth
she hardly stood her
ground. her mongrel dog

died; she quivered with
guilt to know she would
need, then lose, another.

Vultures

In Masai Mara, my footstep burns uneasy
to know this day could mark my grave.
Perhaps I think myself more than mortal
for the sperm I carry but, in truth, I
forget myself, a man of mundane dread
who wrenches to see this dead gazelle.

Why must the dead smell? Or tolerate
these vultures with greedy razor beaks
mining for morsels up her ass? But we
too might screw out our brains and still
die, stink like the mortal joke we are.

Give me your learning; we need to
matter, even as we don't. Our dread
makes us liars to blaspheme the gods of
permanence we aspire to be.

Are we stupid and not evil, after all,
merely a thing aimed at heaven that smells,
a thing afraid? Whatever your name, this is
my dread, my bottom line:

fingers crushed,
knees a bloodied splinter,
two arms at the shoulder severed from my breathing,
a saw through my genitals,
a number inked on my thigh,
my name and heartbeat divided,
my muscle in one belly, my heartbeat in another,
all flushed into sewage as you, like the
mindless vulture you are, eat and shit again.

All this, while nothing of spirit in me reaches
you, a corpse eating corpse without eyes.

On Hearing Gould's Bach
Two and Three Part Inventions

The gills of a fish
and the lungs of humankind
breathe a concentric, musical
will, harmonious and divine.

A dog asleep knows tranquil
ecstasy and cows, who
claim no human reason, prove
their wisdom soundlessly.

The birds invent a gentle
symmetry with the sun. Who would
tamper with happiness to
imitate their song?

From the lake, shore to
shore, the stars all seem
predictable. Yet clearly
some order is their will

and their companion. Thus
every human masterwork
is only a beginning, perhaps
the outset of timelessness

as it pours invention upward
like apprentice to the dew.
Yet our music gives beauty
a name, while fish divide

deep darkness, and music
is what they are but nothing
they desire. Today life is
music, the earth convinces me.

DYING WOLF

The road to your body
is paved and slick with
oil. I hear diesel trucks
along the shore, not the
gurgling of your lungs.

Come, dying wolf.

I will share a new
metaphysics with you,
and curse technology
in killers' hands,

and worship the terrain
your senses made, the
landscape that is yours
for death and nothing
again of man.

I will hunt the hunter
who rides a snowmobile,

the one who runs amuck,
starved in need of wonder,
the one I'd rather
mourn than love.

You will learn another
man's mystery. Your
killer shall die the death
he made for you to die.

THE CLAUDE BERNARD PLAQUE

On the Rue des Ecoles,
a concrete commemoration:

DE 1847 A 1878
CLAUDE BERNARD
PROFESSEUR DE MEDECINE
AU COLLEGE DE FRANCE
A TRAVAILLE DANS CE LABORATOIRE

Beside me the ghost of a dog
wonders aloud:

It must say that Claude Bernard
thought himself a great scientist
and no ordinary man. It must
say he felt possessed by scientific
ideas and refused to hear the
cries of animals or even see their
flowing blood. It must say
he took dogs for living machines
that he cut very slowly into pieces.

Not quite, I answer.

Then surely it describes how Bernard
cut open thousands of animals,
destroyed an organ in each one,
and kept them alive for hours prolonged
and prolonged without anaesthesia,
and how he was mimed in cruelty
in labs all over Europe.

Well no, I answer.

Does it say that Bernard's
teacher, Magendie, immobilized
a small cocker spaniel by
driving nails through her paws
and long ears in order, without
anaesthetic, to saw open
the living dog's cranium and
dissect her spine to expose raw nerves,
and left the puppy, not yet dead,
for use the next day?

It doesn't mention Magendie, I reply.

Does it mention how Bernard,
member of the esteemed Academie
Francaise and hero to France, advocated
in private, without qualm, the vivisection
of human beings, while he continued
to roast living rabbits and dogs
in an oven to their death?

That too isn't here, I respond.

Then what in hell does it say? asks
the ghost of a dog.

It says he worked in this lab
for 31 years.

Paris, 1987

THE CAMARGUE

Twenty miles on foot
through the Camargue,
a prostrate land, austere
design; the wind and a rabid
sun compete for my brain.

I am seeking white horses.
Word has it the herds run
free but they don't: ragged
studs gather to weigh the
curse, another season.
Along the ditch, bushes
bowed like mendicants bear
the howling scoop of
Mediterranean wind above,
gouging gusts, mad and starving.

Then to walk the ramparts
of Arles, nothing more
lonely in this world than
midnight wind in an ancient
town, a river flowing beside
it. The Rhône disappears
out of colour into the night: I
remember the chill Gothic
architecture sends down
the spine, and how we are
alone, with or without God.

Then to bed, in a room of
wooden shutters, Cante
Flamenco rising from the
square into dreams I never
describe that put man and
his death together.

Depression

Talk to me in poetry,
not the dead jargon of counsel.
Hold me close, take me inside you,
and be not an answer but a friend.

I am no hero to my aging bones and,
betrayed without a betrayer, I cannot
wash my skin clean. Still, the
enemies we cannot see are walls
of nothing, you maintain. Then so too

the miles and miles of talk I care
not to know, the incessant canned
laughter and canned sorrow like dead
grass where dogs have pissed, the
words of holy men, their hide and

seek in this world, which is a holy
man's salvation, and whatever the
professional degree then decrees or
concedes to be real. But interest lacks

the means to interest me. The wheel
has broken and I no more care to
exercise the wheel, or talk of healing
my body back to a world that has made
me numb of thinking and hope.

Perhaps you can write a prescription
and make the world more than it is; I
have seen too many dead friends and
buried my heart each time beside them.
Now wine makes me silly; even silly
is a chore. We simply decay and die.

Yet, some days, beneath a clearing sky,
a lie can suffice. And so does a blunt,

severe happiness, or a sorrow that weeps
– and doesn't return – and out into the
galaxy it goes. One day even the pills

do their job; their remedy wears calm
like a jacket and feels nothing. But
must I remind you that depression
is my sanity fighting for life again?

To believe in ghosts, I tell you, is
a sign, but do not desire these spirits
of the dead lest desire become more
lonely. Nor give patience too many
ears to hear mere parts for the whole.

You would have me cursed into
blessing to accept how my life has
done me in. You would have me
reshape my lies and illusions, have
me repaired and hear nothing of the
wound that must be heard – or else

it wounds again. You would have me
listen where every cliché finds a home,
a meal, and a bed to sleep, listen to you
of caw-caw needs, listen to you of
self-inflicted love, and to you of
imposing clarity who see no remedy

that grows inside this dismal gloom
of a mind. What had I offered that, full
of cancer, each one said thanks before
they died? In this fragile sleep that
gives no thanks to waken, and dares
not even dream, I call to them with
gratitude, not to you, the living dead.

A FIBROMYALGIA POEM

In your hyphenated, public diagnosis
(sick-not sick enough), there is no cure.
Nor in the sexless womanizing of poetry,
in a rain check from nine to five, or in a
brief moment when we laugh together and
become one laughter. Nor in the ceaseless
blah blah blah from a voice alleged of brain
that needs to dabble in a guy, or in your abyss
of sincerity, or even in music of armpits hairy
with truth: no, none of these, not then, not now.

In living like a wound, I take much less for
granted now, lest I be granted no drink but the
stale buckets of your polluted well to wash down
these pills and your c'est la vie. But this isn't
your gig and I have no words to talk away these
pains. I must learn again what I am, and not
drown, as before, in this sweet pissoir of a smile
I once named with my name. Each day is another
day aching by, and your New Age wisdom

demands a new punch line, one of joints that
bend very slowly, before I can hear of your
handy mysteries. Should I trust each pill,
each remedy, when many of the many are stupid
in their healing, and their dreaded kindness lacks
a heart to see? We speak the same words, but
these words offer no likeness to muscles that rage,
no mirror to days when I do less and less, though
so much less is too much. You have learned to

defy and cure only the disease you can name,
as you sleep and the world sleeps and thinks
itself not sleeping. So be it: I am no longer an
experiment, no longer condemned to seek healing
of every hand but my own, but remain as
watchful as a grave where death comes now or then.

Quand Le Besoin Est Plus Fort Que La Peur D'avoir Besoin

J'ai peur
J'ai peur de toi
Touche pas mon coeur
Je t'en prie, ne meurs pas

THE AIDS PATIENT

I walk a lifetime to take a piss.
When I shit myself, I live and die in it.

My diet is a megadose of cure,
bottles of pills that ease nothing.

The helping hands are latex fingertips,
the healer a doctor, thinking
or not thinking what to say.

Each morning my body is my voice —
I can't, I can't, I can't —
all bony words without much flesh.
My eye sees dead colour.

One day my lungs will wither to
hollow death and I'll have no reason;

I only lived a very normal life
and still I die from it.

If you were thirsty for blessing,
would you drink from my cup?

If I were thirsty for blessing, would
you, naked, even touch my skin?

Where the labyrinth begins,
the seasons return without you
and, in the margin of daylight,
the sky makes no decision to be.

I am one flesh alive in the death
of another, a balance of will
and the death-hanging sky, and
though we are not formed of destiny,
nor of music that enters silence
like man into woman, it is silence
and the tempo of mountains
that conspire the sounds we imagine,
the way we speak our secrets.

It is silence that makes a step where
every deep question of our subtle,
dying flesh needs a second step
and a pathway of steps beyond.

And if, within the ancient duration
of your heart, there is no safe place,
consider your neighbour. He speaks
a consensus of meaning, yet walks
each step where man is first afraid.
He is evil or not evil, perhaps just
ordinary, just someone else,
and the deepest wound of his silence
calls out to name another. You will

meet him at the circle, you will hear
the part of him where no mercy speaks
and discover he dwells within
the bloodless, empty hollow of your heart.

Do not summon your spirit
of comatose beauty to name him,
but be true to your wounds
and the endlessness of the dead.

Be true to your footsteps and do not
speak your bounty of words that diminish
the incarnate moon, the deep and
darker life beyond these mortal years,
or even the axe and fires of sacrifice. In your
knowledge that is not wisdom, be wise in
silence and make no tally of virgin or youth.
Be still, for, within the labyrinth, each clear
perception proves us blind; each question
proves us deaf to answer. The labyrinth
speaks a silence only silence can endure.

And if you fear the sacred truths you've
heard, whispered among mediocre men,
then make no map for salvation or remedy.
Place your spirit in your footsteps and
let all healing be, even as you walk
within this prism of silence that sings
every dying colour of sound.

But notice, my friend, how even
your terrible death finds the pathway too
dark for walking tonight. Tomorrow,

we will stand, at one instant, between
the path we have taken and the path
we have yet to walk upon, where even
marker stones are the seeds of beginning
and the ghost of what shall be is not
an ending but only a ghost of what we are.

April 13, 2000

ALADDIN'S LAMP

A twenty minute lunch:
two salesmen gulp
hamburger and Coke,
eye the blonde
receptionist walking by.

"I'd like a piece of that!"
laughs one, rubbing his chin.
And genie to his wish,
she cuts off her arm, drops
a bloodied elbow on his fly.

THE CARNIVORE'S COMMERCIAL

Not three square meals
a day, with a portion
of flesh that schools
recommend, because they
abide the meat profiteers,
and not the smiling fool
of a cartoon tuna dragged
from a home, the sea,
and not cartoon hot dogs
seducing your young to a
guiltless fantasy on
Saturday morning TV, and
not the "turkey juices"
that grandpa, the pacifier,
carves on Thanksgiving,
or the sizzling barbecue
that macho, suburban dad
provides to feed his kids,
all would-be men, and not
the movie celebrity, a
legend wearing fur in
yuppie magazines, the
superstar paid in millions
who makes a killing twice,

but you who pay the killer
to bloody his hands, while
you chip in bucks for the
SPCA and, full in the
belly with the dead you
never see, you weep
real tears for Bambi.

THE MAN WHO WANTED A SON

"This favour will make you a man,"
he said, and he kicked me in the groin
as hard as any guy doing a good turn.

Then he offered me his daughter.
She was faceless and serene, elusive
as a field goal falling through a cloud.

The Mermaid That Snored

Seamus, a sailor, the name I was born
I've lived days of fortune and lived days of scorn
Come sit down an hour and listen to me
How I once loved a mermaid beside Scotland sea

As I was out sailing to Iona to pray
The winds took my boat, near the rocks I did stray
I spied a fair mermaid upon the sand
O save me, I cried, ere my boat scrapes the land

Her hair was like sunlight a-sinking at night
But it wasn't this fire that gave me a fright
For she was a-sleeping while the waters did roar
And like depths of the deep, this mermaid did snore

I promise you my heart, I promise you gold
Stop this mad storm, or make my ship bold
But like the great cannon I'd heard in the war
The storm all around her, this mermaid did snore

So I crashed on the rocks like raindrops in May
My heart was a shipwreck, nor words could I say
'Twas then she awoke, 'twas then touched my brow
She said, "Lie down a while, there's no danger now."

And when I awoke the sky was as blue
As the wind in her voice and this story is true
But the mermaid is gone, my heart is full sore
I'd give the lark singing for the mermaid that snored

LES ARENES

A carnivore's sense
of humour. The surrogate
Nazi, a tourist from Chicago,
asks me, a vegetarian, to
choose between a confused,
tormented bull and my
hypothetical daughter. As
if I were a Gypsy or a Jew
nursing twins, insensibly
compelled to decide
the skull he'd crush underfoot.

Let this be plain: when
the elegant matador's knee
starts to quiver, I shout
"Good falling of guts!"
and cheer the bull. I drag
a spectator, idly diverted
by death, to crude butchery
on the curb and carve his
belly for the wandering bitches
on the Boulevard des Lices.

Then I light a candle in
the church of St. Trophime
and consider the contagion
of human curiosity. The
flickering light imposes a
grin on the skull overhead,
centuries old and pockmarked
with time, carved when
angels had leisure time to
jostle for standing room on
the head of a picador's pin.

Arles, 1978

FOR SAKE OF A MEMBER

The brave explorers of Europe
sailed off, on angry seas, for spices:
spice preserves meat, said my
schoolteachers of history.

But in truth, these searchers of old
craved aphrodisiac, for peppers,
cloves, and cinnamon were said to
keep man erect, a penis everlasting.

They butchered the Indians of
Mexico for chocolate, another
aphrodisiac. Gold in wooden ships
was a bonus—and a censored reason

that school kids understand. But
chocolate was too bitter and the trade
in sugar and black slaves began.

Today, the manly explorers of
Toronto venture the streets of
Chinatown for the gallbladder of a
bear, an aphrodisiac say the ancients.

And so, the carcass of this bear, with
a thousand of his kin, rots in the
wilderness, all because this laughable
thing called man would kill his
brother and ruin the earth to stand tall .

A HOUSEWIFE

She slices a tomato,

imagines her wrist
diameters of flesh,

nibbles the bug-less
unchewable skin.

She has eaten her arm,
spit out the bone;

it's her husband
she broils in the oven.

MY BONES TROUBLE ME

My bones trouble me, my joints ache afraid.
I journey too far, unbelieving, to reach meanings
I once understood. My anger burns worn out embers.

Still it burns to behold the wondrous elephant
beaten to stand on one leg, or the dolphin
made brainless leaping through a loop. At the zoo,
the circus, the rodeo, the bones of animals bend
in human hands. But, no matter their esteem,

the masters are baser animals, the watchers stupid
and obsessed with toys. Whatever my own treachery,
I wish their hands broken and cast aside in pieces.

Never mind the sage who declares men are wise
to kill other animals lest they choose a hatred to
murder their neighbours instead. When the deer
turns her eye toward the hunter's rifle,

when a hunter's rifle makes the man, the sage
has seen murder, not a caring, merciful God.

If wise men forsake the world, the rest all get
even in some lousy way. And those who give
no mercy still ask for mercy and conjure hell,

where others burn before eternity burns. They
record their tedious meanings in volumes of shit.
And some are consoled, as we demand of animals,
that the debts we pay in life are not the debts we owe.

Words From A Cancer Ward

I
They send an intern to tell me:
"It's cancer." Mumbled ice water
splashed on my face. My nightmare

remembers me, my horoscope
laughs, the intern turns to escape.

II
Fourteen get well cards the first week.
Then nothing: duty visits, half-hearted
grins, they smile and back away.

May I laugh, shed tears?
What's etiquette for cancer?

III
Visiting hours, a Muzak of smiles.
And chocolates, potted exotic plants
I cannot use. Over my skeleton of veins,
they tell jokes, play buffoon, kill time.

I gulp water and burp, strain to hear
the chit-chat detouring death. Then,
ignored, I go crazy and lie still.

IV
I'm the sum of his fears, the
book he put aside twenty years
ago, unread. He works the day
shift, seven to three: he feels
betrayed. The kids accuse him

with silence, he eats supper
from a can. And daily he
squirms to visit his balding wife.

JAMES STRECKER

V
I confess my legs are thin, my withered skin
too heavy for an arm, my breath a stench no
mouthwash can erase. I confess I gasp for air

to rise, I moan a bloodless chain of complaints
around your battered sleep. I confess I broke my
vow to die after you, scraped your macho

innocence. I confess I demand the courage you
fear to know and hunger to need you, need you.

VI
They wash me at five a. m.
Then intravenous for breakfast
and a bedpan the nurse forgets at noon.

Would I like to sit up?
Would I mind a tube down my nose.
Do I have the spare change my husband
needs for the meter outside?

VII
Take home your magazines; even with my
glasses they blur. Speak louder: I can't hear

the question you asked yesterday and asked
a few minutes ago. Don't pretend I'm cured

or almost well; stop reaching half way. Find
my doctor. Why does he mutter past?

VIII
Naked for one man all my life. Now a
team of doctors and students measures
my belly. The interns practice concern,
note my decay on a chart. I want nothing
after death; I hope we truly die.

IX
Doctor, my tongue pukes a salty taste
I'd rather starve than eat.

 It's the chemo.

Doctor, my toes feel icy and numb,
I hobble on rubbery knees.

It's the chemo.

Doctor, I cannot sleep through my dreams,
I count footsteps at 2 a. m.

It's the chemo.

Doctor, I'd rather die than rot away
my life day after day.

It's the chemo.

XI
In our home we kissed at Christmas
and birthdays. We never spoke of
cancer, even colds. We knew tomorrow's
weather and all the football scores; in
June we planned a holiday.

Our kids graduated, their habits aged.
And now I sleep alone beside a metal
cane. O, someone, cradle me.

You Are What You Eat

An illiterate witch
might boil our bodies together

you, a summa cum laude
bat, of scholarly radar,
exuding doctored intellect

until my skeleton's contour
bounces back, but not my
pliant skin or emptiness.

I, too, in the cauldron,
mindful of your learning
by degrees, benumbed and

baked by your erudition,
bloodless afloat in repartee,
sensing a thesis in your touch.

Maybe the fire will cackle
ironic laughter below as we boil
and gel together, a cliched

gummy mush one nowadays
calls intimacy. But I swear
on the League of Ivy, my

bookish one, a serpent will
dangle above your Ph.D and

applaud the hooks and wires
we use to enjoy each other.

VIVISECTION AND THE CAT

vivisection says
    come talk some cat
and cat says
    meow and wow, somebody's real

and vivisection says
    no cat's good stuff all the way
and cat says
    cat's all cat and you're wrong

and vivisection says
    mankind's number one
and cat says
    then let him cut you up and check you out

and vivisection says
    I burn cats alive for science
and cat says
    I didn't volunteer, so why you telling me?

and vivisection says
    my boy needs a heart transplant
and cat says
    no, you need a new heart

and vivisection says
    life's supposed to be pain
and cat says
    wisdom's another way of not giving a shit

and vivisection says
    I need meaning to fill my darkness
and cat says
    leave me be, it ain't my fault

JAMES STRECKER

and vivisection says
    I can stop us from dying
and cat says
    prove to me you ain't already dead

and vivisection says
    people live longer today
and cat says
    just so they can kill kill kill kill kill

and vivisection says
    I want to help the world
and cat says
    fuck it, just be kinder to cats

and vivisection says
    you cats kill really mean
and cat says
    at least I don't pretend I don't

and vivisection says
    you cats torment birds and mice
and cat says
    so do you and you napalm people too

and vivisection says
    I'm gonna drill your brain
And vivisection says
    I'm gonna drill your brain

A "Virile" Art Form

In a Spanish abattoir, the novice
matador takes time to rehearse. He
thrusts his sword, again and again,
through the flesh of captive cattle
waiting to die. The matador perfects

his art; the cattle take a very long time
to die; the stab wounds overlap. At the
Running of the Bulls in Tecate, Mexico,
a wild-eyed bull foams at the mouth.
Young men on horseback drag his

exhausted body, flesh on gravel, to the
corral. The spectators, for reason a
devil knows, poke him, pelt him with
bottles and rocks, spit on his fear
because he hesitates, he hesitates to

die. The mob of men, aroused by
helplessness, potent with the spirit
of a gang, laugh aloud with manly
disgust. Could they know their
manhood is a lie, like all heroic lies

that need blood to come easy? So,
Picasso, did you sketch the bull made
ready for the ring? They beat him,
hurled sandbags on his spine, pushed
vaseline into his eyes, injected his

battered fear with sedative, ground his
horns to a blunted, harmless nerve, all
lest he, the bull, fight back. Did your
hand ever doubt and freeze with the
outrage of a Guernica or even a mute

compassion? Did you sketch the
blood thirst or only the blood? And
you, Hemingway, did you smile and
applaud the thrice-repeated ritual?
The bandoleros maimed each

shoulder until the bull was a helpless
foe for matador's childish elegance.
When they shredded the bull's neck
muscles with pick and lance, did you
pity the bull tormented to his only

death, drenched in the bloody hue of
national sport? O, man of painting,
man of words, could you be silent at
this slaughter, call your art manly, and
even applaud? And Lorca too, was it

geometric duende or a coward's
butchery that you described in perfect
words? Were you cowardly, like the
mob, to conceal your thirst for blood
and name the reason art? If you three

be men, let us spare the bull; let
us drive this darning needle through
your own testicles. And as you scream,
from pain, not the olé of before, let us
marvel at the manly art you make of it.

A Day In The World

Her mother, her father,
and the whole village watched.
The soldiers ripped off her clothes
and they lay her infant beside her.

Then four soldiers raped her, one
by one, as her hungry baby cried
a useless cry. When they were done
and she was dead, though living,
when no man of the village would
touch her again, she asked to feed
the baby at her breast. A soldier

with a knife cut off her child's head
and gave it to her. At last she went
mad. This is today, not sixty years ago.

And this is today. Our neighbour, the
scientist, who lives nearby, locks two
rats in a cage, gives them fifteen thousand
electrical shocks; they lick their feet
that smoulder and go crazy. And this:

the research scientist shaves a beagle
pup, covers her with gauze and
kerosene, and sets the living dog afire.
And this: a research scientist beats
monkeys on the head with a
hammering device and poses one
monkey for the camera as she laughs.

And another monkey is shot above the eye.
Like a mother, who lives beyond the Adriatic
Sea, a mother who cannot imagine what else
men will do, she cannot die soon enough.

THE NOBLE BEAST

Let us retell the fable of the noble
beast. The lion strangles or suffocates
her prey, a long and agonizing death
for the wildebeest. Her cubs chance
often to die abandoned and starved,
or killed by other lions. The females

hunt and the male claims feeding
first, yes we know, but most often
the lion is a scavenger, eating rotted
carcasses left by hyenas, wild dogs,
or disease. That lions kill only what
they need for food is a deadly lie
to the wildebeest brought down
to feed vultures and not the lion.

But the lion speaks no hypocrisy,
no morality, no collective guilt
that uncages mankind to torture
when killing would do. The lion
reshapes no perfect god to justify the
knife he uses too easily, too well.

No, I would not be black-skinned
or diseased and starving in Africa
while the world looks away. Nor
would I be a Jew to endure the
smiling fangs of humankind; a
holocaust begins anew in every smile.

No, I would not be in your hands,
whatever your reason, religion,
humanity or name. You do what you
do; your God of mercy, who forgives
your every deed, comes after.

INEFFABLE BEAUTY

To create the pigment of roses
for your cheek, living rabbits were
clamped in a vice; their eyes were
burned away.

I have no word
to compare your skin to petals

A DEAD GULL ON OMAHA BEACH

At the Gare Routière
of Arromanches, empty
Parisian buses kill time.
Local Normandy women beg a
mini-skirted style , too contrived
for the Calvados coast. In twilight
they saunter nowhere and back.

On a tank wiped clean of carnage,
Norwegian kids take absent-minded
aim, eat sandwiches of ham,
synthetic red, while an American
tourist remembers his youth,
weeps for school chums four
decades late: "Their name was

Jankowski, two brothers, both
quit high school to join, never
came back." Then he whispers
an apology, a heresy in Washington,
his home: "Some people will call
me a Communist for this, but
the leaders are to blame for war."

Along the coast, among nine
thousand waist-high monuments,
American graves, children from
New York play tag. The dead gull
on Omaha Beach, a bird no longer
putrid, just dead, soars waterlogged,
over time, on comatose sand.

Bayeux, 1985

TERRY FOX

I could not see Terry Fox,
like a resolute, one-legged bird,
on his run for cancer research.
The air was too polluted

with gaseous fumes and metal
dust, too thick with poison
vapours that keep our livelihoods
burning and spike us with

cancer. And most of the
local citizens were too busy
to cheer this gutsy young man,
running into legend, anyway.

The kids were downing
hamburger with the works; this
meant chemicals they couldn't
pronounce. The populace at

large was smoking its passive,
collective lungs to rot or dying
from the air beneath copper
coloured skies. And research

scientists, intent and curious, were
deeply buried in another wonder
drug to bless disease the hunger
for money had wrought,

drugs like Thalidomide,
Cyclophosphamide, Oxychinol, or
another researched miracle cure
that kills in the name of healing.

TEMPLES

On vacation one decade apart,
my two friends, Raymond and Bob,

both returned from Oriental temples
seasoned with millennium, temples

washed porous and clean of holy war
and bloody, holy daggers, temples

carved sacred for Hindu, Buddhist,
and Jain, and for gods of every hour,

speak only of temples overlooking
classy restaurants. Inside, in the

shadow of temples, where no life
is spared, hands made ingenious

by centuries, sew the lips of a living
monkey together, push the monkey's

skull through a hole at centre table,
saw off the monkey's crown, and sip

fluids from the live monkey's brain
through a straw, a delicacy they say.

PEASANT LAUGHTER

Without an honest word
to conceive my death,
or a god unbound enough

to fuse me with my kind,
I forego religion the best
I can and sin with the trees.

I grieve my tearless dead,
touch their callused, forbidden
tears, their dregs of the
barrel dreams, and sing

the peasant's unshaken will
bartered for sugar and flour.

Some drank a back door into
heaven; some paid their
way into an open grave with no

change to spare, in the next
life rather dead than
poor to starve again.

What name makes them holy?
chattel bought and sold
with hogs they tended
or two-fisted peasantry,

raging in their smiles, who
took God's will in the teeth

and chose to die unchosen,
their laughter a phlegm
they spit on the rich
yet subtle as a willow.

KATE TROTTER'S ALMA
for Kate, in Summer and Smoke

We are made
of nothing certain
and shadows
fused with mourning
dream for us.

Yet for reasons
told a broken heart
it is sometimes
easy to live
and parched
of bloodied waters
to thirst again
what drinking blood
would have us know.

We are granted
the art to make
salvation of wounds,
give anguish carved
by godless will
an echo and a cry,
though we die
mad with reason
or only mad.

So here it begins,
monarch like a
hopeless heart
that cuts the night
in two. She weaves
a wordless meaning
to spoken sound, she

labours to birth,
and the yearning

moons of summer
crash broken
in her eyes.

THESE I REMEMBER

The yard is clucking with chickens.
The old man, my grandfather,
is a teller of bedtime stories.

He seizes a brown hen near the coop
and holds the bird's legs, and an
axe, in strong, indifferent hands.

The stump of a tree is a wild criss-cross
of scars and then it is bloody. The boy
watches killing he has seen before;

he remembers a greasy soup on his
tongue and, later, where he plays, he
finds the dead chicken's head in a ditch.

After many years, he eats no meat;
after many years he discovers a wounded
bird. Perhaps the sparrow is too mangled

to live, or perhaps he dreads wounds,
cannot forgive the bird's broken wing.
Perhaps he hates the sparrow's need of

tending in a day too busy for pity. But we
are only our deeds, without prophet or
saviour to forgive what we do, and now

he remembers the sparrow frozen still,
staring through his eyes, until this very
day, as he brought the heavy shovel
down upon the sparrow's skull.

A Special Hell

If evidence be true, the vivisectors among us
need a special hell: one for men once dead to
compassion and now in need of it, men of
unbending logic, now honest in despair, men
supreme in cruelty, now worthless to conscience.

Witness Claude Bernard, schizophrenic and
manic depressive at the end. Or his colleague,
Blanchard, who, blind and dying out of reason,
implores his family to remove the ghostly eyes
of cats he has tortured that surround his bed.

Or Flourens, successor to the esteemed Bernard,
roaming his final days in the Jardin des Plantes,
howling and barking like the dogs of remnant
dignity that he bolted down and carved in his
laboratoire. Or John Read with cancer in his
nerves, the very nerves he poked in living dogs,
who writes, "This is a judgment on me for the
pain I have inflicted on animals." Alas, these

men of barbaric logic, now men of madness and
remorse, can no longer tally the progress of their
science: 200 million animals tortured in labs in
1991 around the earth, and 4,221,801 experiments
on living animals, with British license, in 1983.

Or explain how pesticides were tested 32, 979
times, or the medical wonder that came of killing
932,335 rats. Or describe the colours of wing of
251,818 laboratory birds or explain how men of
science would endure psychological stress,
burning and scalding, electric shock, or
interference with their brain and parts of the
central nervous system, or electrodes, held by
brother scientists, upon their nerves of deduction.

What Did You Eat?

What did you eat
this evening?

The limb of a calf
who never saw light

who stood in one place
unable to turn,

each morning the
birthing of pain,

more pain, and confusion,
for ninety-five days

until you cooked
anaemic flesh

and prayed over dinner
to a god who might

save your children from
such human indifference,

not even because they are
human, but they are yours.

Consider your children,
then; their bodies have not

moved three months until
now. Their flesh is tender,

white, soft as water.
It's all a matter of taste.

And You Call Me Naïve

as you defend vivisection,
your neighbour punches the face
of his wife into pulp,
he buggers his child daughter,
and his belly's become a sewer of
many thousand cows and swine that
died, and he didn't give a damn

as you defend vivisection,
a pilot drops napalm on schoolyards,
gas in the lungs of cities far away,
while a soldier burns peasant
genitals with voltage enough
to light a starving town, while
a president stockpiles the world's
end for God his personal saviour,
he says, and for corporate payola

but when man the scientist
enters a lab, you explain, he
becomes a creature of moral finesse,
a man who carves his own heart
in the victim he maims, and not a
man who clings to his prestige,
his power, his funding, his job,

not a man who enjoys the helpless
tied down, while his hunger to know
makes nothing of his indifference,
sees no reflection in eyes too numb
with pain to whimper or to scream.

A Woman's Masterpiece

She reads a volume
of her life,
caged in marriage,
caged in prose.

A stranger lurking
and foreseen
steals her child
from the crib,

writes a woman's
masterpiece
for the bookshelf
in the hall:

daughter bruised
behind an alley
garbage can,

clothing ripped
from infant skin
page by page by page.

FAMILY ALBUM

My father. The factory laid
invisible welts on his back,

drove him into the concrete floor
until he made jokes that smelled
of iron dust, dreamed of fishes,
the stream long dry.

My mother, Anastasia, dispatched
among rigid, breaking immigrant
spines. At ten she could love
no more the blushing child's

movie screen, and lamented her
own mother's drudging decay,
vassal's wage, a slave, like a
horse, in Pennsylvania.

My farmer uncle, stinking and
content, a lifetime of harvest
tallied on
his skin, his arm that
thrashed anything coarse or gentle.

Look at the pages
I have no secret to conceal.

My people carried the rich
on nameless sagging backs
until they saw the world in black
and white, then yellowed with
age like photographs.

The Five Last Words

Do not enchant this human breed
where they pillage holiness,
or cover their ruin
like spring, false spring.

The animal kin they destroy
sing loud their own human flesh,
yet they would have it so.
Their hearts have truly perished.

And father, forget them,
for they know what they do.
They have killed and are killing
the mother of gods in you.

MELINA'S SONG TO THE MOUNTAIN
for Melina Kana

What song have I to persuade your desire?
What song that solitary winds would lift my hair
like a cloud of wordless memories
over the harbour,
that I would burn my lungs to ash
if I should climb your secrets,
and higher still, to ease your solitude?

What words have I that decree your words?
What words that speak your flesh the sky caresses,
words that know the wisdom
of boulders colliding,
and words like no words at all
that die beyond the sky
when the mountain's desire is my destiny?

What words have I to sing your mountainside
that erupted with gods many seasons ago?
Yet, as each autumn dies like melody,
the gods all stand still to listen
to my song. Or is it only a valley they hear
where I fell to sleep and
dreamed my footsteps dancing away from you?

The Squirrel

The squirrel fastens
September to March,

stuffing his cheeks
full of nuts and seeds.

I take this glutting
of a belly for esoteric

laughter; the squirrel
girdles his heart with fat,

gilds a death he can't
foresee. Verdant leaves

abstract into autumn.
The squirrel chatters

near a tree, teases
Sumitra, our patient

cat, of scythe-like spine
and cool, implosive eyes.

MARGIE'S DANCE FOR CHRIS

Woman in black, a raven's cry silhouette:
not death in silence that mimes all music, all words,
but a dance to drink a potion of his meaning,
a dance like all the widows of man,
childless again and their own flesh taken away.
This wound has raged a humble wisdom in her
though, perhaps, the dead are deaf to what they were
or the death of a spirit is not the soul itself,
as she turns and turns like the world and all its days.

Woman in black, gracing the arc of sorrow:
her fingertips shape the love that is punished for love
and, infused with the fierce and infinite shadow
that heals the wound and then the healing,
she buries her cry in a sun-rising sound elsewhere
and dances what flesh can make of flesh no more.
Into all of emptiness, this fisted angry dance,
and her eyes are full of him and endless sight,
full of love that echoes home when uncalled love is given.

Woman in black, in secrets that make her be:
a naked motion born of the endless heart
unshrouds all meanings married to his death
and the dancer, deepened like an answer into herself,
gestures in time what knows no reason, no sense of time.
What art have we to make our grief less mad?
What answer? No answer, to the will of a moon-breasted sky
that tempts our love to more than love and to nothing,
like moments that we remember that maybe never were.

for Margie Gillis, in memory of Chris who died of AIDS

CANALE GRANDE
for Barend Schipper

The most descended of places
where water, mated everlasting to the sky,
consumes a mind unmoving stillness
and hues of morning light beckon to reason
like fingertips divided by clouds
that sail in time –or is it imagination?
And again we shall hear beginning,
the serenity of laughter that knows
in every memory a reason to live.

The watcher aspires a distance from himself
and, if we are not blessed, we become,
we remain, miraculously what we are,
and even more because our silence
loosens the binding curses of heaven
and hell. A dream goes looking for dwelling
on this canal, although words cannot name
the nameless; words can only wait
beside a silence that is.

No one listens and no one speaks
and every answer the heart desires must die
unfinished and unknown upon these waters
where wisdom provokes no mark. On this canal,
the earth makes ready for the moon, orphan
to the lunatic needs of humankind, until the
human will disturbs our sleep no more and
a destiny, composed of dreaming, waits and
waits like water that decays and also dreams.

THE ANSWER IN A DREAM

This morning, I drove northern roads beside a
livestock truck. The trailer's side was a wall of
impassive, sturdy metal and animal flesh, calves
inhaling their first and last morning of light. The
trailer's rubber tires whirred a rapid "schnell, schnell,
schnell," on the pavement, because, so it seemed, all
mad efficiencies are human, sadistic, and the same.

And later, we came upon hunters at twilight. They
carried traps and hatchets, flaunted a predator's
private joke in their smiles and, drunk with beer or
killing, I could not tell, pointed at their prize: coyote
and muskrat, heads askew, with eyes like jewels in
a crown of death. Something of flesh, like my body,
was a killer; something of flesh, like my body, was
dead. And lest these hunters be not cursed, I cursed
them in silence, for they held the blessing of life
and its ending, even my own, in eager, dirty hands.

In twilight, what did it matter how killing began? Maybe
man plowed the earth until the need of food made him
hungry for blood; maybe a woman's society ate berries
and no animal's flesh. What mattered the beginning,
if man is still a killer out of hand, of mercy inconstant,
of thinking decayed? What mattered the dread of
impotence, of death, if man still breeds the cowardly

killer that is? And you who explain, I envy your words
of divine mystery, your meditated serenity that sits
away from the world, your gentle reluctance to know
what others must endure, and sometimes even your ease
to join in the butchery that nature decrees. Awake, I
truly love a few and, with evidence of mercy, wait for
my kind to curb his savage art. But in my dream, I
despair that he tortures, for no reason, what is holy if
anyone is so. Then I shoot him, I shoot him in the face.

WASYL SZEWCZYK

This method I learned
from Charlie: After the meal
wash your bowl and spoon.
Let them dry on the counter
until you eat again.
Be patient.

He was a bachelor. In his seventh
decade they brought women, like
weather-beaten cattle, to the timid
man's home for him to take in
marriage. He rejected the sagging
Polish widows and their match-made
schemes for his land.

He left the house and garden in a
will. There was little else: four boxes
of novels describing sophisticated
bachelors and accessible blondes,
and a handful of age-ruined
photographs, the girl beautiful in 1921.
Had he loved her? He wanted to nod
his head yes, but couldn't. He left

an epithet, Charlie, a handy anglicized
substitute for the alien Wasyl.

We removed two kinds of shirts from
his room: white shirts covered with
cellophane, then dust (these should not
be spoiled too soon by common
labourer's use), and others laden with
sweat, odors of work eating the fibres.
He wasted nothing, not even his life.

Wasyl Szewczyk is dead,
Wasyl Szewczyk of Galicia,

a Ukrainian serf from a feudal age
who despised the priest and his
landowner's god. He had seen a
pregnant girl beaten by holy fists, had
fled to a dirty coal mining town, a
fourteen hour shift, and wept from
the pain of his burned, bandaged hands.

His fingers learned to play the clarinet,
cut hair with a barber's expertise, hold
a book of Shevchenko's poetry. He
was attuned, like spring, to the delicacy
of creation. At meals, he belched with
thanks, for bread and cream, a peasant.
He lies buried in Beauséjour, Manitoba
where he once pastured cows, and his hair
was black as a rain-soaked prairie field.

Wasyl Szewczyk is dead.
There was little to say after him. We
lacked his wit–was it peasant or Slavic?–
that taunted death as a nuisance and friend.
He knew the dead to be lucky.

What aspect knows the man?
He posed unsmiling for photographs.
He lived a long life, should have hated
the world. He wore a suit on Sundays.

Charlie Szewcyzk, the farmer
Wasyl, died last April in his
eightieth year. At seventy-five
he had learned to play
the violin.

JAMES STRECKER

POEM TO THE EARTH

I have no words
to charm you, the earth;

my voice is not perfumed
of clay. And to love you
I must drink your gentle water,

drink or drown in it,

though I, with wounds
to which we are born,
would crush this day of sorrow
between our thighs. Like a

woman unrelenting in desire
your breath becomes a fleshy rose;

and all eyes of the world
at once, all eyes and my
lonely desire, behold your

branches for the very first
time. I reach to touch that
faraway place, where you drink

my secrets dry, and every word
I speak makes love to you.

A SOLSTICE OF MUSIC
for Beth Nielsen Chapman

Wear the sun's music and dance as
before, although, for reason of winter,
a chill runs deep where death comes
again to the dead. A whisper of
darkness caresses the eye and again
light makes no shadow through the
dead, the dead we had loved, perhaps
the best we could. The wheel of seasons
rolls easy again. They are dead;
they make no shadows dance.

We too will die one lifetime short of
summer, but, for now, we are happily
mortal. The sun plays midwife to our
senses, even as our bones age and bend,
like music that drifts incestuous upon
its ending. May the sun dream roses
into being, as we sing, and sing loud
again, the travellers through our flesh
who stood defiant when the world
pounded many suns out of them.

How mortal are we to imagine a
kindred fire in the sun? How
immortal to defy the despairing want
of light? When love is born of no
beginning, though in love that's
taken we also die, we touch our dead
slowly once again. And in this
darkness, seduced from time, they
touch our skin, the way one spirit
caresses another, like a secret. No
need of angels here, where love
becomes a greater love. Still we know
these angels' blessings one by one.

BREL, LE DERNIER DISQUE
for Guy Martel

Condamné dans un miroir
bourgeois, mon corps qui chante
pour cracher son mépris, meurt sans
dormir des rêves comme une feulle
prête a tomber dans les goutières

d'une mémoire. Qui fait l'amour
sans folie, qui pleure sans sagesse?
Qui garde la liberté de mourir selon
son goût? Dans la brume, dans
l'habitude, je vomis le sang de
mes rêves.

          Ainsi la terre se parle,
se répond: le coeur, c'est une pierre
jetée par un dieu absurde, d'une
jeunesse dure, sans avenir, déjà mourante.
Regardez les nuages gris, les nuits qui se
caressent, nuits après nuits, jamais
divisées par le soleil tout nu dans son
chagrin. Seul, j'écoute un fleuve coulant
vers sa propre mort, esclave de lui-même.

Enfin, on joue sans visage, même dans
la mort. Le corps se trahit et trouve
dans son sang un rose déjà sèche.
On oublie tout sauf l'amitié, tout sauf
la dignité aux genoux cassés.

BESIDE THE HEMLOCK GARDEN

They are made of metal, the
collar and pressure bars. They
squeeze the bear secure in a
coffin cage. He cannot move.

All day, a catheter pierces
the bear's gall bladder and
feeds a machine. He strains
his tongue to lick water
from the bars. Beyond a
small opening, the food he
hardly can reach teases him.

Very soon, the bear goes
crazy, mutilates his body,
tries to kill himself the best
he can. But his keeper makes
him live and each day his
bones grow more deformed.

The pain is something you
must try to imagine. In China,
ten thousand bears live fifteen
years in agony this way, all
because the bile from a bear's
gall bladder is used for
aphrodisiac, used for shampoo.

And beside the hemlock garden,
you consider suicide, perhaps
blessed in wisdom to know
the one you must kill, the one
already dead, the one beyond
mercy who needs to die?